SandCastle
Let's Go!

LET'S GO
BY
HELICOPTER

ANDERS HANSON

Consulting Editor, Diane Craig, M.A./Reading Specialist

ABDO Publishing Company

Published by ABDO Publishing Company, 8000 West 78th Street, Edina, MN 55439.

Printed in the United States.

Editor: Pam Price
Curriculum Coordinator: Nancy Tuminelly
Cover and Interior Design and Production: Mighty Media
Photo Credits: Shutterstock

Library of Congress Cataloging-in-Publication Data

Hanson, Anders, 1980-

    Let's go by helicopter / Anders Hanson.
      p. cm. -- (Let's go!)
    ISBN 978-1-59928-898-7
    1. Helicopters--Juvenile literature. I. Title.

    TL716.2.H363 2008
    629.133'352--dc22

                                        2007014937

SandCastle™ Level: Transitional

SandCastle™ books are created by a team of professional educators, reading specialists, and content developers around five essential components—phonemic awareness, phonics, vocabulary, text comprehension, and fluency—to assist young readers as they develop reading skills and increase their general knowledge. All books are written, reviewed, and leveled for guided reading, early intervention reading, and Accelerated Reader® programs for use in shared, guided, and independent reading and writing activities to support a balanced approach to literacy instruction. The SandCastle™ series has four levels that correspond to early literacy development. The levels are provided to help teachers and parents select appropriate books for young readers.

Emerging Readers
(no flags)

Beginning Readers
(1 flag)

Transitional Readers
(2 flags)

Fluent Readers
(3 flags)

SandCastle™ would like to hear from you. Please send us your comments or questions.

sandcastle@abdopublishing.com

Helicopters are a type of aircraft. They have spinning blades that control their flight.

A helicopter's controls are in the cockpit.

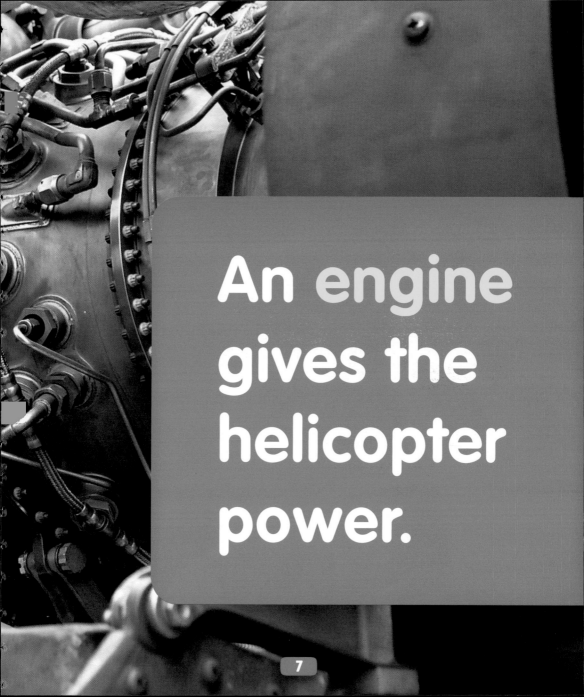

An engine gives the helicopter power.

Spinning blades on the main rotor lift the helicopter.

A smaller tail rotor turns the helicopter.

Helicopters have the ability to hover and land in tight spaces. They are important tools in many rescue operations.

This helicopter
helps put out
a forest fire. It
drops chemicals
that slow down
the fire.

16

Military helicopters have many roles on the battlefield.

Helicopters are used to check traffic or take aerial photographs.

HAVE YOU BEEN IN A HELICOPTER?

WHERE DID YOU GO?

TYPES OF HELICOPTERS

attack helicopter

heavy-lift helicopter

light helicopter

medium-lift helicopter

utility helicopter

Twin-rotor helicopters have two main rotors that create lift.

The word *helicopter* comes from the Greek words *helikos*, meaning "spiral," and *pteron*, meaning "wing."

In 1942, Igor Sikorsky built the first mass-produced helicopter, the Sikorsky XR-4.

GLOSSARY

aerial – from or in the air.

chemical – a substance made or used in a science experiment. Also, a substance made by chemistry.

cockpit – the area in an aircraft, boat, or car that contains the vehicle's controls.

hover – to stay in one place in the air.

rotor – a part in a machine that rotates, or turns, inside another part. In a helicopter, a rotor is the blades and the parts that hold and rotate the blades.

To see a complete list of SandCastle™ books and other nonfiction titles from ABDO Publishing Company, visit **www.abdopublishing.com**.

8000 West 78th Street, Edina, MN 55439 • 800-800-1312 • 952-831-1632 fax